A Year on Monhegan Island

TICKNOR & FIELDS BOOKS FOR YOUNG READERS • *New York 1995*

A Year on MONHEGAN ISLAND

BY JULIA DEAN

AUTHOR'S NOTE

Although the rhythm of life on Monhegan Island is constant from year to year, many of the specific events in this book took place between December 1989 and November 1990, and all of the photographs were taken during that time.

Acknowledgments

My sincere gratitude to the residents of Monhegan Island, Maine, who became my friends and welcomed me into their community. A warm thank you goes to school teacher Beccy Chamberlain and her six students for the wonderful times we shared; Raquel and Peter Boehmer for making me a part of their family; Newt Searls for providing a winter roof over my head; Bryan Hitchcock for his continual assistance; Cynthia Krusell for sharing Museum information; and Harry T. Bone, Mary Beth Dolan, Billy Boynton, Jackie Boegel, and Barbara Hitchcock for their neighborly help. I also wish to thank my friends for their support throughout my project, especially Bud Pagel, Beth Barrett, Steve Potter, Harry Kaste, Carole Peet, and Ashley Rogers. Finally, I would like to express a very special thanks to my editor, Kimberly Olson Fakih, and publisher, Norma Jean Sawicki.

Published by
Ticknor & Fields Books for Young Readers
A Houghton Mifflin company, 215 Park Avenue South, New York, New York 10003

Manufactured in the Singapore

Book design by Tom Starace
The text of this book is set in 14 point Adobe Caslon

TWP 10 9 8 7 6 5 4 3 2 1

Library of Congress Cataloging-in-Publication Data
Dean, Julia
    A year on Monhegan Island / by Julia Dean
        p. cm.
    ISBN: 0-395-66476-4
    1. Monhegan Island (Me.)—Juvenile literature. [1. Monhegan Island (Me.)—Social life and customs.]   I. Title.
F29.M7D43   1994
974.1'53—dc20   93-24534   CIP   AC

For the Monhegan school kids:
Orca, Kila, Kristina, Livka, B. J., and Ben,
who have enriched my life.

M onhegan Island is a dot on the map due east from the central coast of Maine and ten miles out to sea. In the summer, Monhegan is crowded with hundreds of visitors, while winter brings isolation to the small community; in 1990, only seventy-five people lived there year-round. Spring and autumn serve primarily as transitional periods, as residents open up thc hotels and stores for summer and then close them down for the winter.

Winter is a time of solitude and tranquility. Strangers appear only rarely. On the bitter-cold days when residents stay close to home, the road through the village is often deserted. There are no cars on Monhegan; the only vehicles are the few trucks used for local industry.

Winter's isolation generates a community spirit in which traditions thrive. The one-room schoolhouse has always been central to these customs. Since 1847, the white wooden structure has stood on a little hill at the north end of the island, facing the main road. During a

An aerial view of Monhegan in its entirety, looking north.

Monhegan's one-room schoolhouse.

period in the 1960s, there were so few children on the island that the school was closed. The townspeople felt the loss, however, and voted to keep the school open, even when there are fewer than five students. Below that number, the state of Maine does not require self-governing regions to provide a local education.

With the exceptions of a new Formica countertop, a carpet, and the addition of indoor plumbing, the school has not changed since it was built. Between the front door and the door leading to the main room is a hallway for coats and boots. In the classroom, a chalk board covers the east wall; a solid wall of windows faces west. An oil stove at the front of the room provides the heat; at the back is an American flag and the platform stage used for so many community

events. In between are the students' desks and one computer, which the children share.

In 1989, Beccy Chamberlain came from Augusta, Maine, to teach at the school. Her third-grade son, B. J., brought the student population—grades one through eight—up to six: B. J., Ben and Kristina Murdock, Kila and Orca Bates, and Livka Farrell.

For Beccy's students, a typical school day began when they recited the Pledge of Allegiance, and after someone fed the praying mantis.

The school's six students and Beccy Chamberlain say the Pledge of Allegiance before the school day begins.

Kristina Murdock (left) and B. J. Chamberlain share a book during school reading time at the library.

Math, writing, reading, spelling, and grammar followed. During morning recess, the children played games in the school's front yard or down on the beach. At lunchtime, the students went home to eat, then returned for an afternoon of science and social studies. Throughout the day, everyone studied the same subject at the same time, although they used textbooks appropriate to their grade levels. Beccy walked around the room, helping each student.

The children of Monhegan are familiar with life on the mainland. They visit relatives in other states and go to large cities to shop or for school field trips. Yet living where there is little traffic and no crime gives them more freedom than they would have in many places, and their days are full. Still, they sometimes wish for things they do not have, such as fast-food restaurants, movie theaters, a playground, and a wider choice of friends. "We get tired of each other," said ten-year-old Kristina Murdock in 1990. "We'll have bad days and good days. Sometimes we'll fight nonstop just about dumb things." When they need to get away from one another, they read, watch movies on their VCRs, play Nintendo, or walk in the woods.

Surrounded by the sea, the children are familiar with its dangers, as well as its beauty. They grow up hearing the island's stories. At seventy-seven, Rita White still remembered a tragedy that took place in August 1926. It was a beautiful day, Rita said, and from the village the sea looked calm. But on the east side of the island, the "back side," the waves were pounding against the rocky ledges. A girl named Jacqueline, who had spent all her summers on Monhegan, was having a picnic with her friends to celebrate her eleventh birthday. She was sitting on a flat rock, far from the ocean's edge, when a big wave rushed in and pulled her out to sea. Her fifteen-year-old friend Edward plunged in to save her, but both were dragged out by another wave and drowned. In memory of the two children, the residents built the Monhegan Memorial Library, adjacent to the school. Especially during the long winter months, the library is an important part of life on the island.

Every year, from mid-December until just before Christmas, the schoolchildren carry on the traditions begun by earlier generations of students. The first custom of the Christmas season is the search for the schoolhouse Christmas tree. In 1989, eighth-grader Orca, as the oldest student, took charge of the annual event. All six children, bundled up against the icy weather, ran ahead of Beccy and into Cathedral Woods. After scouring the woods for twenty minutes to find the perfect tree, they took turns using a two-handled saw to cut through its trunk. The tree was so large that three children had to carry it through the woods and up to the schoolhouse.

With Beccy's help, the children made decorations for the tree and

Cathedral Woods

*The students carry their Christmas tree
to the schoolhouse after cutting it down.*

Livka Farrel decorates the school Christmas tree.

the classroom. They also practiced the play that they would perform later in the month at the community Christmas party. They constructed props and designed costumes; by the night of the party, they were ready.

For as long as anyone can remember, every resident of the island has been invited to the Christmas party. On the given night, at about six o'clock, islanders wander down the dark road carrying flashlights and dishes of food for the potluck supper. The people in the noisy, crowded schoolhouse settle into a muffled silence when the lights go down and the performance begins. Final bows are followed by much feasting. The evening ends with a visit from Santa Claus, played each year by the resident with the roundest belly. As tradition dictates, he hands out gifts to the children, who sit on his lap one by one with their wish lists. The community gathers once again, on Christmas Eve, for a candlelight church service. There is no preacher on the island, so the residents organize the service themselves. Christmas Day is reserved for private gatherings.

During the week following Christmas, the community prepares for Monhegan Island's next important winter event: Trap Day, the launch of the six-month lobstering season and the day when the fishermen first set their traps. It usually takes place on January 1, unless the weather is bad or someone is sick. Despite every fisherman's desire to race for the best fishing grounds, if any one of them is ill, they reschedule the event. On Trap Day nearly everyone on the island helps. Setting traps is such a big job that the fishermen could not do it alone.

Trap Day.

Driving old beat-up trucks, the fishermen travel down to the wharf through the early morning darkness with their final loads of lobster traps. They add these to the heaps that have been gradually piling up during the previous days. Each fisherman has his own special-colored buoys to distinguish his traps from those of the others, and each has his own spot on the wharf where these traps—up to 600 for each fisherman—are stacked.

Trap Day.

At sunrise, the rest of the community comes down the steep hill to join the fishermen. By this time there are only narrow paths among the towering piles of traps. The residents form lines along these paths and pass traps down the wharf, like a fire brigade passing buckets of water to a blaze. In the frigid salt air, each boat captain waits his turn to pull up to the wharf, where his crew takes the traps from the nearest person in line and loads the boat.

The deck of each boat leaving the wharf is covered with traps stacked seven high. The fishermen, dressed in bright orange and yellow oilskins, speed out to various spots around the island, anchor the traps, then hurry back to the wharf for more. Again and again, traps are sent down the line toward each waiting crew. This activity continues all day long without ceasing, although the residents take turns retreating into a little shed on the wharf to get warm or to gulp down homemade food. The work does not stop until all the traps are set.

For hundreds of years, the island fishermen had lobstered all year long, but around 1907 they asked that the Monhegan season be shortened to six months. The most common explanation for this request credits the fishermen with a desire to conserve the lobster supply by allowing the lobsters six months in which to grow and multiply. Another explanation suggests a policy prompted by greed. Those who fished

Fisherman Bryan Hitchcock measures a lobster to check that it is of legal size.

Alfred (left) and Sherm Stanley unload bait.

elsewhere in the summer worried that while they were gone, the whole crop would be harvested by those left at home. Consequently, they petitioned the state legislature for a closed season, which was granted.

"Whether the reason behind it was virtuous or not, the plan has worked well," said Vernon Burton, who at seventy was still working his traps. "If we fished year round, then things would soon be fished up and we'd be working for nothing all the time."

In all of Maine, Monhegan fishermen are the only ones who trap lobsters from January through June. Most of the state's fishermen begin trapping in the spring and quit when the weather turns cold, for winter fishing in the Atlantic Ocean is no easy task. Biting winds, freezing temperatures, and pounding seas test a crew's strength and endurance. But Monhegan fishermen prefer the shorter season. They earn more for their hard work because there is little outside competition. The season also gives them time to pursue additional jobs, such as carpentry, tourist businesses, or other types of fishing.

Lobster prices have increased since Monhegan's veteran fishermen —Alfred and Sherm Stanley, Vernon Burton, and Doug and Harry Odom—returned to the island in 1946 after World War II. Back then, lobster brought forty-five cents per pound; in 1990, it brought ten times as much. Other changes are also taking place in the lobstering industry. Women are fishing now, like resident Zoe Zanidakis, who is called a fisher*man* on Monhegan Island. It is not an easy job for a man or a woman. Technical improvements have made lobstering easier, but it remains backbreaking work.

"The old wood traps were hard to haul," said Bryan Hitchcock. "They were heavy, and they were a pain in the neck because of the rocks. Wire traps stay where a wood trap would have been destroyed.

The fishing boat Desperado, *at sunrise.*

All the boats are different. The electronics are different. You can tell how much kelp is growing at the bottom. The next thing you know, we'll be able to see the lobsters crawling down there."

Yet the technical advances have made fishing an expensive occupation. Like the price of lobsters, the costs of boats and equipment have skyrocketed. "It's practically prohibitive now to buy the boat, gear, and stuff that goes with it," said Sherm Stanley, the fourth of six generations of his family to live on the island.

Other prices have risen, too. Some newcomers, eager to settle permanently on the island, have had to leave when they could not afford to buy property. Houses on Monhegan cost $100,000 or more, compared with $3,000 in the late 1940s. This is largely the result of out-of-state people buying houses to use as summer homes. Without new permanent residents, the population could dwindle, though not for the first time. Doug Odom, the oldest of two bachelor brothers who arrived on the island as teenagers in 1930, remembers a time when the population shrank to nineteen. Then it grew again. His brother, Harry, said, "It will go down, hit bottom, and start right up again. It's done that for years."

Artist Jamie Wyeth's house on a winter day.

Residents admit that winters are difficult. The restaurants, inns, and shops that are open during the tourist season close by October. With the exception of fishing and an occasional construction job contracted out to one resident by another, work is scarce. Temperatures drop below zero, with steady winds and turbulent seas. The town water supply is turned off for five months a year, so each household must maintain a cistern or well.

The social life during the winter is limited. Friends take turns hosting dinner parties during the week, and on Saturday nights the residents usually gather at the Monhegan House hotel to play bingo. People meet at the wharf when the mail boat arrives three times a week. Often they help the crew unload the cargo. Since everything used on the island must be brought over from the mainland, deliveries can include not only mail and groceries, but washing machines, lumber, and even trucks. After the boat has been unloaded, residents socialize at the post office or at the grocery store, which is open only on the afternoons of the days the boat arrives.

But the residents believe that the benefits of living on the island make up for the hardships. "I like the people," said Bryan Hitchcock. "I don't love them all. They don't love me either, but it's like a big family out here. We know so much about each other that we take care of one another. You're not going to get let down out here if you need something."

Top: Captain Jim Barstow helps unload an appliance from the Laura B.

Bottom: Part-time residents play cards in the post office.

Peter Boehmer, whose house is not electrified, works on his battery-powered computer by the light of a kerosene lamp.

Raquel Boehmer moved to the island in 1967 with her husband, Peter, and their three young children. They liked the isolation, she said, because it allowed them to have a strong family life. Peter earns his living as a carpenter, and Raquel airs a live weekly radio program called "Whole Foods for All People," which is broadcast over Maine Public Broadcasting Network. Additionally, they produce two desktop-published newsletters. Like the Boehmers, many who settle on Monhegan are looking for a way of life rather than for careers and work a variety of jobs.

For other residents, such as the Stanleys, Wincapaws, Days, Burtons, and Rita White, Monhegan Island has always been home. "You feel safe here," said Rita, who once went seven years without going to the mainland. "You don't have to lock your doors and you could walk up and down the road all night if you wanted and nobody would bother you. You're not afraid of being mugged. When you're in the cities now, you don't know who's coming to grab your bag or bop you over the head."

But living on Monhegan demands self-reliance, independence, and resourcefulness. The island is not for everyone, especially not for those in poor health. There is no doctor. The islanders have learned to handle most crises themselves. When a child got a ball bearing stuck in his ear, Alfred Stanley used a magnet to pull it out.

Still, common sense will work for some calamities but not for

Billy Boynton.

A town meeting in progress.

others. Someone who is seriously ill or injured must be taken to Port Clyde by boat, and from there to the nearest hospital, a twenty-minute drive. In an emergency, residents call the fishermen on the island, whose fast boats can make the trip to Port Clyde in thirty minutes in good weather.

The residents' concern about health care resulted in the founding of the Monhegan Emergency Rescue Service. The first summer the Rescue Service operated, its members had little training. "We called ourselves the Band-Aid group," said Faryl Henderson, "as that was about all we were qualified to do." By the following year, they had been trained by professional health-care workers from the mainland and earned their state licenses. Since then they have given first aid to people suffering from heart attacks, strokes, and broken bones while rushing their patients to the mainland for further attention.

The residents are accustomed to taking care of themselves and of the island. On September 4, 1839, Monhegan was named a plantation, a form of government set up by the state of Maine for communities smaller than a town. Since then, "We run our own school, set our own tax rates, and make our own decisions," said Billy Boynton, Monhegan's first assessor, or "mayor," as he jokingly has been called by his friends since taking office in 1981.

Sometimes debates are informal. "We'll talk the problems over in the post office," Bob Boody said, "and although we won't solve a thing, we'll certainly feel better." But when a controversy must be settled, Billy and his elected committee organize a public meeting. Every year-round resident of legal age has a vote. These meetings deal with such ongoing issues as the deer population and the leashing of dogs.

In the 1950s, nine deer were brought by boat to Monhegan Island. Residents were excited, but as the deer have multiplied and grown tame, opinions have changed. Many people think of them as pests that eat or trample gardens. Others, such as Harry T. Bone, whose pal "Honey" comes to his door for snacks, think of them as friends. Some islanders argue that the deer should be sent back to the mainland, others that they should be killed, and still others that they should be allowed to remain on the island. As a result of this controversy, it is now illegal to bring any kind of animal but a house pet to the island.

Left: Harry T. Bone feeds his friend Honey as she makes her daily visit.

Right: Deer at sunrise during a Monhegan summer.

Another debate concerns the leashing of dogs. During the summer, when the population increases substantially, some residents worry that the dogs will attack someone. Others are against a leash law and believe that their pets should be allowed to run free. The present law states that dogs must be leashed, but in the winter it is ignored.

While the issues on the island differ from urban concerns, they are nonetheless important. Underlying the specific disputes is the residents' interest in protecting their way of life. Even the decision to bring in telephones and electricity changed Monhegan considerably.

Prior to 1983, residents did not have private telephones, although pay phones were available. People remember standing on the porch of the Monhegan House hotel at Christmas waiting in the cold to use the phone. Strong winds and freezing temperatures kept their calls short. In addition to this inconvenience, high seas often broke the underwater phone cable; when it broke in 1981, the islanders were without telephone service for two years.

Some islanders did not mind living without telephones; others did. Faryl Henderson, who in 1990 helped Josephine Day manage the Trailing Yew inn, remembers that, without a telephone, all the businesses that served meals had to write to the mainland with their food orders. They had to plan grocery lists ten days in advance, so that the mainland stores would have time to receive orders, fill them, and

Breakfast time at Mr. Vics in Monhegan House.

arrange for the food to be taken to the boat in Port Clyde. When a restaurant ran out of an item such as sugar or steak, the cook would have to borrow from a neighboring restaurant.

There were those who feared that telephones would threaten their peaceful existence, but in 1983 the community sued the phone company, which had resisted providing service because of its high cost. The islanders won, and that same year a microwave tower was erected on the lighthouse hill.

In the past, the community had decided against bringing electricity to the island. By 1984, however, some residents wanted more modern conveniences. That year, electricity became available through a private company started by Sonny Remick, a lifelong islander. Before then, most people had obtained power from generators, which often broke down, occasionally started fires, and always intruded on the quiet of the night. And generators were not always convenient. Someone watching a television powered by a generator might have to rush outside during a commercial break to refill the gas tank.

Yet convenience comes with a price. The private company charges more than Maine's public service, and some families live too far away from the generating plant to take advantage of the service. There are still residents using gas-powered generators, solar-powered batteries, and kerosene lamps.

If, despite these changes, life on Monhegan Island is more peaceful than life on the mainland, the pace picks up in the spring. By March, all the islanders are busy preparing for Monhegan's summer. Spring, a season of transition, passes quickly, yet it has its own special character and traditions. The temperature is cool, the melting snow has turned roads to mud, and the 200 species of island flowers are still two months from blooming when the Easter celebration takes place. On

Spring brings fog and muddy roads.

People gather in the Island Spa for their usual morning cribbage game.

that day, before dawn, all the children and adults of the island hike to Burnt Head, a 140-foot cliff facing directly east. There they sit in silence to share the sunrise. Then they go to the Boehmers' for a breakfast of Raquel's homemade doughnuts, coffee, and baked goods made by the guests. Breakfast is followed by an egg hunt for the children.

In April, Billy Payne returns from his winter home in South Carolina to re-open his store, the Island Spa. For more than sixty years local residents have congregated at the Spa, which Billy Payne leased in 1985. Billy—who remembers talking for hours with the Spa's original owner, Zimmie Brackett—strives to carry on the traditional spirit of the store.

More than 100 cups and assorted hardware items, as well as a multicolored dinosaur mobile, hang from the ceiling's wooden beams. A red stained-glass lobster shines brightly against the eastern window. The wooden shelves display canvas hats, rain ponchos, sweatshirts, paper products, office supplies, paint, books, and old black-and-white postcards of Monhegan scenes that were photographed by Zimmie.

When Zimmie was in business, he stocked gifts to sell to tourists, but Billy does not. "I didn't want to cater to the people off the boats," Billy said. "They were walking in, buying something, and walking out without any contact. It was like being a vending machine." But visitors who do stop at the Spa are always welcomed and included in conversation.

Summer cottages and other businesses begin to open soon after the Spa does. By Memorial Day, the owners of the Island Inn, Trailing Yew, and Monhegan House have readied their rooms for rent.

For the children, the last day of school marks the end of spring and the start of summer. Sometimes the school year closes with an eighth-grade graduation, although with so few children graduations are rare. The year Orca Bates graduated, Beccy Chamberlain arranged a surprise.

Jamie Wyeth (left) hands Orca Bates his diploma.

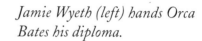

Jamie Wyeth, a third-generation painter from the famous family and a part-time Monhegan resident, had painted a series of portraits of Orca over the years, and they had become good friends. At Beccy's invitation, the artist flew to Monhegan by helicopter in time to hand a diploma to Orca.

The end of eighth grade marks a turning point for every child on the island because Monhegan has no high school. Many of the children have said they were ready for a change, but the transition to high school is always difficult.

"The only thing that prepared me for high school," said Heather Boody, "was the fact that I knew I was going." She and her former island classmate, Tigger Hitchcock, used to worry about the changes they would face. "We were anxious to get off the island," Heather said. "We were getting bored. But we were very nervous."

Heather adapted well, but not without pain. When she played soccer her freshman year of high school she would return to her room in tears. "I didn't know how to be competitive," she explained. "When we were growing up, we had to be careful of the little kids. When we played kickball, we had to tap the ball—everybody had to play fairly. I would frustrate the kids at Gould Academy because I would let the other people take the ball away. It's good to be fair, but being aggressive is good, too, and I missed out on that."

Monhegan Island in the fog.

Heather and Tigger believe Monhegan's school system gave them a good education. But while they enjoyed the challenge of high school, they also missed the island. On the mainland, Tigger said, "there was always some noise—the lights buzzing, or the cars going by. You could never shut your eyes and think that you were back on Monhegan because you could always hear something that told you you weren't."

Students return home from mainland schools on holidays and in the summers, but rarely in between. The distance is a hindrance, and unpredictable winter weather makes it impossible to guarantee that a boat will be able to make the trip both ways. The island children experience at a young age what most American public-school students do not face until college: searching for schools, awaiting acceptance, leaving home, adjusting to roommates. Their early departure from the island also puts a financial burden on their families. Private boarding schools are costly, but there is no other choice, unless the child has relatives living near a public school.

The children know about this expense and begin working when they are young. Ben Murdock owned his first lobster trap when he was four. At six, he had fourteen more and had saved $95 by working periodically with his father, John. Other children baby-sit, and, in the summer, wash dishes or wait tables at the restaurants, stock shelves at the grocery store, or start their own businesses. Through the years, the children have set up road-side concession stands. Orca Bates has

People arriving on the Laura B.

paddled tourists over to Manana (the tiny island off Monhegan's coast) in his father's dory. Tigger Hitchcock bought his own truck and used it to transport baggage on the island. These can be highly profitable jobs during the months of July and August.

By then, summer cottages, inns, and guest houses are full, and the island's population has increased by 600 people. Monhegan is a different place.

"There's that first wave of people who come, and you sort of have an initial reaction of resentment," Billy Boynton said. "The island used to be yours. Your sense of privacy is gone and suddenly you are on display again." But, he added, "If Monhegan had the same seventy-five people year-round, it would be a very small and isolated place, and I don't think, for me, it would be as attractive a place to live."

Billy Payne, who is always one of the first to greet the newcomers, agreed. "One of the blessings of the island is the cycle. By the time you want to see somebody new, a whole bunch of people show up. It's nice."

Visitors walk up the hill toward the Island Inn.

Every day the captains navigate their tour boats slowly into Monhegan's tiny harbor—past shoreline cottages with big wooden porches, and alongside the weathered wharf, where a crowd of people waits to greet friends, pick up supplies, or take the return trip inshore. Three battered trucks, backed in a line close to the ramp, are loaded up with baggage, groceries, and mailbags. Everyone walks eastward up the steep road. Some stop at the Island Inn. Others continue down the hill, past the Lupine Gallery, to the Island Spa, which faces west along the main road. Billy Payne points them in the right direction.

Visitors wander through the village, past a large meadow, a shed covered with posted notices, a pizza shop, and neatly stacked lobster traps. The dirt road, so barren in the winter, is crowded.

There are two types of summer visitors on Monhegan: the cottage owners, who return year after year and establish close friendships with the residents, and the tourists, who come for a short time.

Summer visitors began coming to Monhegan in 1878, when a

Notices posted on the rope shed inform visitors of local events and places to visit.

woman named Sara B. Albee opened a boardinghouse. Artists came first, then vacationers. By the early 1900s a summer colony had been established. Some of America's major landscape painters lived and worked on Monhegan, inspired by its beauty. Robert Henri, a prominent figure in the New York art world, stepped ashore for the first time in 1903, and many of his artist friends followed. Rockwell Kent, the most famous of these, visited for the first time in the summer of 1905. He became so entranced with the island that he developed insomnia and could not stop painting. Other well-known artists who have visited include Edward Hopper, George Bellows, and John Sloan. Winslow Homer also made the trip out, but, according to a local story, he got seasick on the ferry ride over and took the next boat back.

Throughout the twentieth century, artists continued to form a major part of the summer community, but the prices of real estate and hotel accommodations have risen so much that most artists can no longer afford to buy homes or go there for extended periods. The artists' colony is disappearing.

Monhegan also attracts the visitors that the islanders call "day trippers." After World War II, Earl Fields, then the captain of Monhegan's mail boat and ferry from Port Clyde, began making both morning and afternoon trips. This allowed tourists to come out on the early boat and return to the mainland the same day. Now three tour boats a day go to Monhegan—from Boothbay Harbor, Port Clyde, and New Harbor. Together they make five roundtrip excursions each day during the summer, carrying 150 or more "trippers" at a time.

Tourism is an important part of Monhegan's economy. Most of the residents make their living from it and look forward to the summer season. Doug Odom, who operated the grocery store with his brother

A Monhegan visitor paints the view across the meadow.

Harry for forty-nine years, has said, "I always thought the more people the better." But not everyone agrees. Most people would prefer to limit the number of summer visitors.

Sometimes the year-round residents rebel. In 1987, when one of the boat captains added an additional excursion, Billy Payne closed the Island Spa early one afternoon. Outside the store he hung a sign that read POPULATION EXPLOSION, protesting the increased numbers of tourists. Other islanders agreed with Billy that the boat operators were exploiting Monhegan.

The residents' concerns about the large summer population are realistic. Monhegan's ecology is delicately balanced. Too many people might use up the natural water supply, wear out the paths, and create a problem with garbage, which must be hauled inshore at considerable expense. The increased possibility of fire is also a major threat. Although smoking is prohibited in the woods, visitors do not always obey the law.

In 1987 some of the residents hired an attorney to look into legal ways of controlling the number of tourists coming to the island. The islanders learned there was none. Like cities and towns, plantations are considered public domain, where people are free to come and go. Since then, however, the numbers have leveled off. The extra boat was stopped, and some rainy summers have kept people away. For now, the

"Day trippers" leave the island on the afternoon boat.

A bird-watching group follows the trail along the cliffs.

residents' fears have been put to rest.

While most people who come to Monhegan love it, some do not. There are no nightclubs, tennis courts, big hotels, swimming pools, or shopping malls. "We've seen golf clubs come off the boat, and high heels," Billy Boynton said. "They really didn't know what they were getting into."

For most visitors, though, the island is a lovely place to escape the pressures of the city and to enjoy a gentler pace. During a visit to Monhegan with a birdwatching group, Juliet French, an eighty-year-old woman from Gloucester, Massachusetts, hiked all seventeen miles of the island's trails. Her only other visit had been in 1936. "It made an impression on me and I just had to get back," she said. "It's been worth waiting for."

The physical appearance of Monhegan has not changed much in the more than half-century between Juliet's two visits, largely due to the efforts of Charles Theodore Edison. The son of the inventor Thomas Edison, he formed the Monhegan Associates, Inc., in 1954. It is a corporation of homeowners whose goal is to "preserve for posterity the natural wild beauty...of the so-called 'wild lands'...as well as the simple, friendly way of life that has existed on Monhegan as a whole." Edison gradually acquired parcels of land that were then put in a trust designed to preserve the island in its natural state.

Without the foresight of Charles Theodore Edison, the cliffs of Monhegan Island might well be lined with houses, hotels, and condominiums, and the forest might have been cut down. There certainly would be too many people.

By Labor Day there are signs that the season is changing. The summer cottages have been boarded shut. Each day another boatful of people leaves the island. Following a custom, residents who accompany departing friends to the boat give them flowers to throw overboard as the *Laura B* pulls away. If the flowers float back to shore, the islanders believe, the person leaving will return.

The year-round residents have mixed emotions during this transitional time. They are sad to see their friends leave, yet they look forward to fall and winter. Most are ready for the change of pace. "I like having mixed seasons," said fifth-grader Kila Bates in 1990. "You can be alone for a while and then have lots of friends. It would be nice if it

Edwin Jahn waiting to leave the island after a summer visit.

Alfred Stanley repairs traps in preparation for lobster season.

were cut up into fourths so you wouldn't have to wait so long or have too much of one thing at once."

But Monhegan's yearly cycle is well defined. Winter is long and often lonely; summer is busy and goes by quickly.

Autumn is different on the island than in the rest of Maine, where thousands of tourists visit to view the brilliant fall foliage. On Monhegan, the crowds have gone home and the evergreens stay green. Of the visitors who do arrive, most come to attend the painting workshops given by resident Don Stone or to observe the 300 species of birds that stop on the island during their southern migration. By Columbus Day, even these visitors have gone, and all the hotels and restaurants have closed.

This is Sherm Stanley's favorite time of year. "After you've been here for years," he said, "you get tired of the same questions over and over and over, and it's just such a peaceful time of year when things slow down and the weather is still nice."

During this period, the residents begin to prepare for winter: They get wood from the mainland for their stoves, and hay to bank around the bottom of their homes; they clean and prepare their cisterns before the town water is turned off; and they seal windows against the winter winds. The fishermen service their boats, fix traps, bag bait, and paint buoys.

Before winter sets in, the islanders observe their autumn traditions. A night or two before Halloween, the students put on a play for the community. Then, on Halloween itself, the children meet at dusk, wearing costumes they have made themselves. Guided by their flashlights, they walk from one end of the island to the other, visiting every household. The children have learned what to expect from each home. Some people distribute homemade baked goods; others hand out candy bars bought from the limited selection at the grocery store. One year Raquel Boehmer gave out toothbrushes.

In November, Billy Payne closes the Island Spa and returns to South Carolina. Only the post office, grocery store, and Shermie's fish house are left as places for the residents to meet. Although each fisherman works in his own building, Shermie Stanley owns the fish house

During a school party, four-year-old Cat Bates learns how to make a jack-o'-lantern from fifth-grader Kristina Murdock.

overlooking the harbor, and people gather there at the end of each winter day. Inside, a cribbage game is always under way. Green-and-white buoys decorate the ceiling, and on the walls hang tools, kerosene lamps, old faded photographs, and other memorabilia. The room glows with yellow light from a bare, dangling bulb, while outside the weather grows colder.

Winter has arrived.

Shermie Stanley (left) and Carl Wincapaw play cribbage in the fish house, while Sonny Remick (seated) and Alfred Stanley watch.